MW00904320

Welcome to "Vision Board Book for fam...
designed to turn your dreams and g... ...reality.
Elevate your vision board experience.
Packed with over 640 carefully curated images, it offers more
inspiration and motivation than ever before.
This is your best vision board book yet to achieve your aspirations and
manifest your dreams.

Our vision board book is designed for family and community
gatherings(for male and female). Each book can accommodate up to 4
individuals (20 pages and 160 pictures), featuring separate sections
for everyone. Here are some useful tips on making the most of this
book:

**1. Share Your Visions: Before dividing the book, gather
together and share your visions verbally, jotting down notes
as you go.**
2. Division: Divide the book among the 4 participants.
**3. Image Selection: Each person selects images for their
vision and checks if others need any of those images, then
tears and shares accordingly.**
**4. Vision Board Creation: Each individual personalizes their
vision board by placing the chosen images as they see fit.**
**5. Vision Sharing and Gratitude: After completing their vision
boards, participants share and explain them to the group,
expressing gratitude to those who shared images.**

Through this vision board experience, participants not only set personal
goals but also practice communication with others and understand each
other more deeply. Furthermore, even after the party ends, they can
collaborate to achieve their goals and build a unique support system.
Our vision board will illuminate your future. Cultivate your dreams and
make them a reality together.

I love MY FAMILY!

Family is where Life begins

Thank You

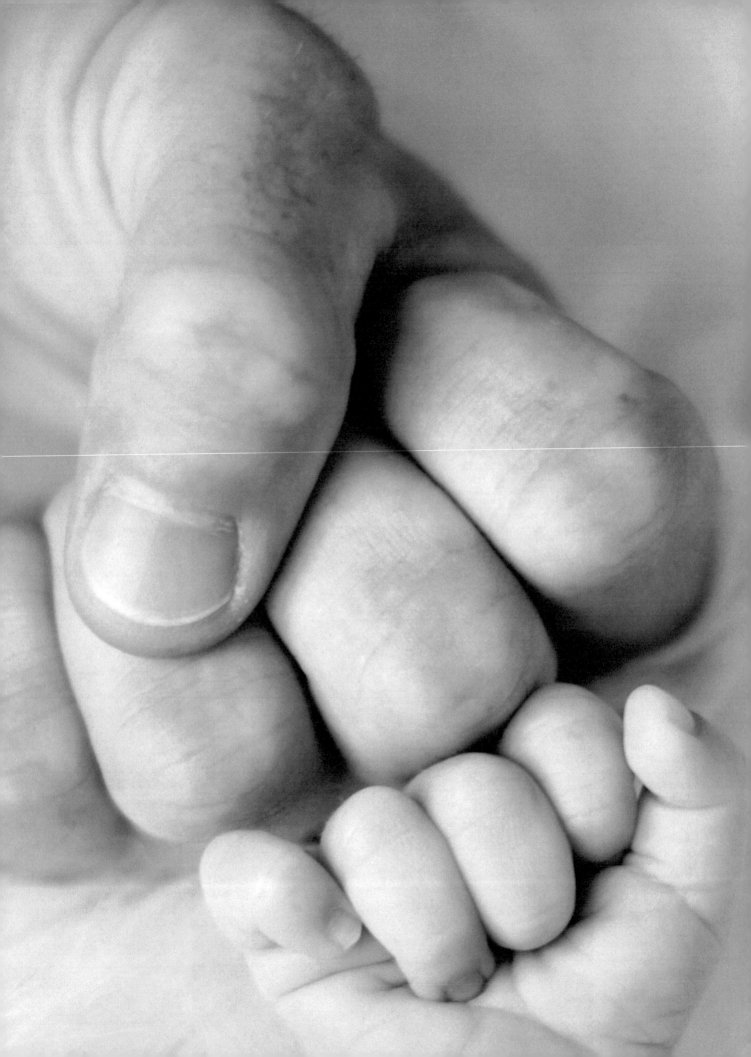

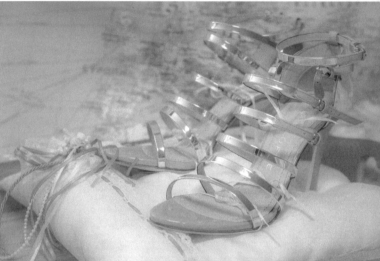

Bon Appetit

Laurence Graff

i love you

HAPPY
MOTHER
DAY

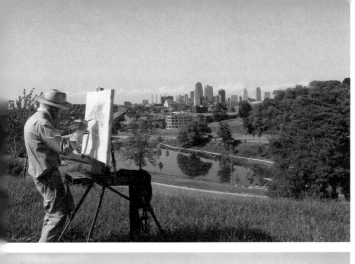

French Korean Spaninsh

ENGLISH

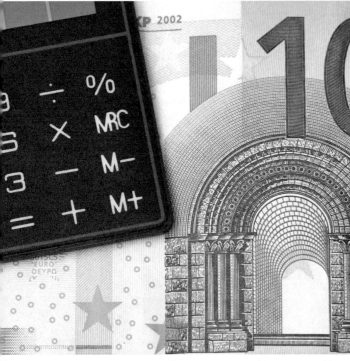

I

love

MY

FAMILY!

Family is
where Life
begins

HAPPY MOTHER DAY

Thank you

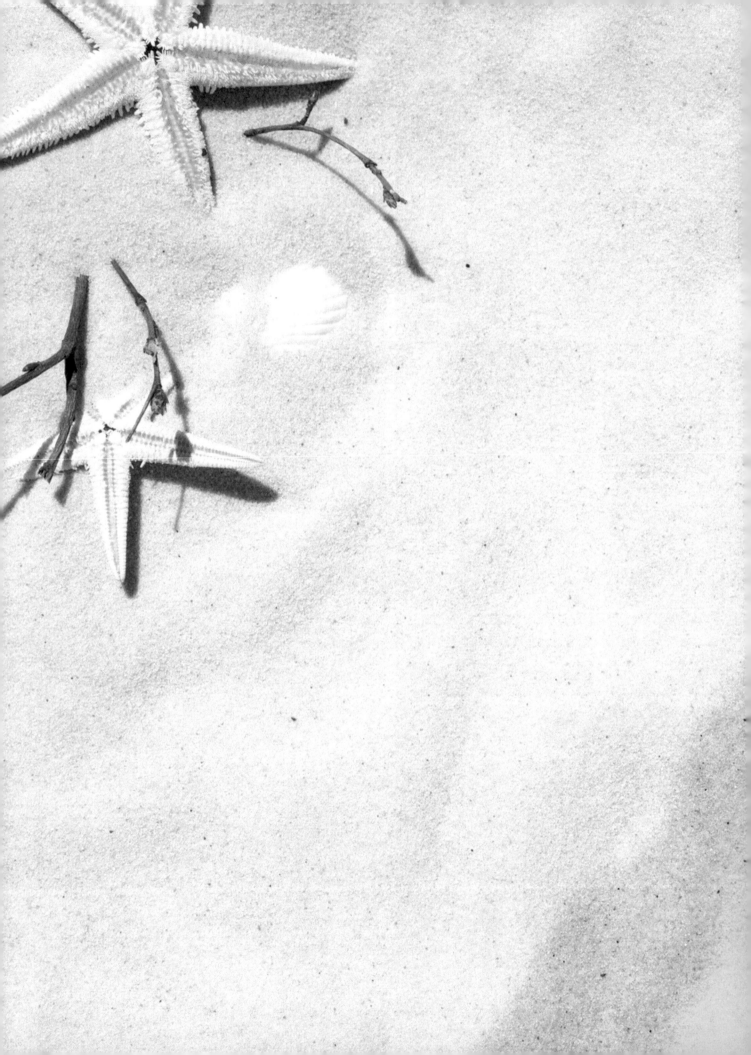

I love MY FAMILY!

Family is where Life begins

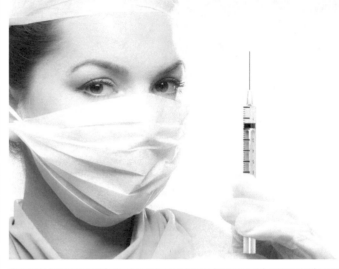

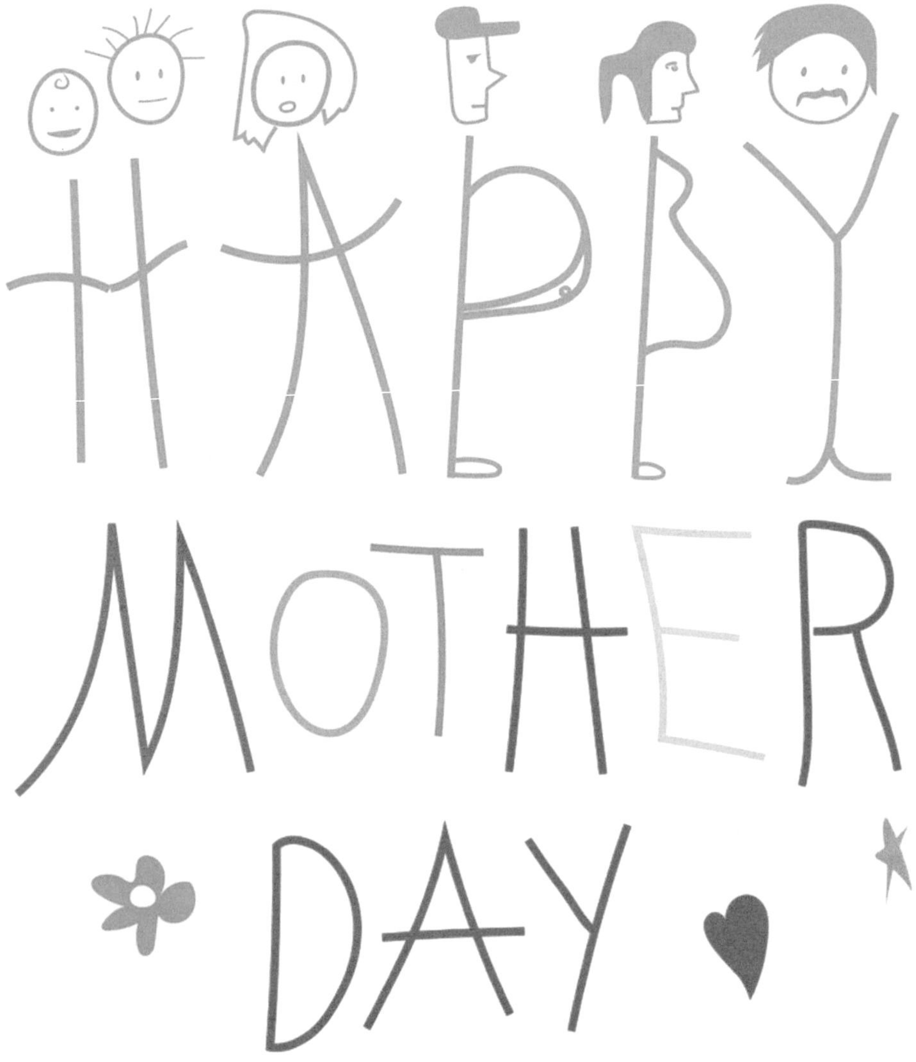
HAPPY
MOTHER
DAY

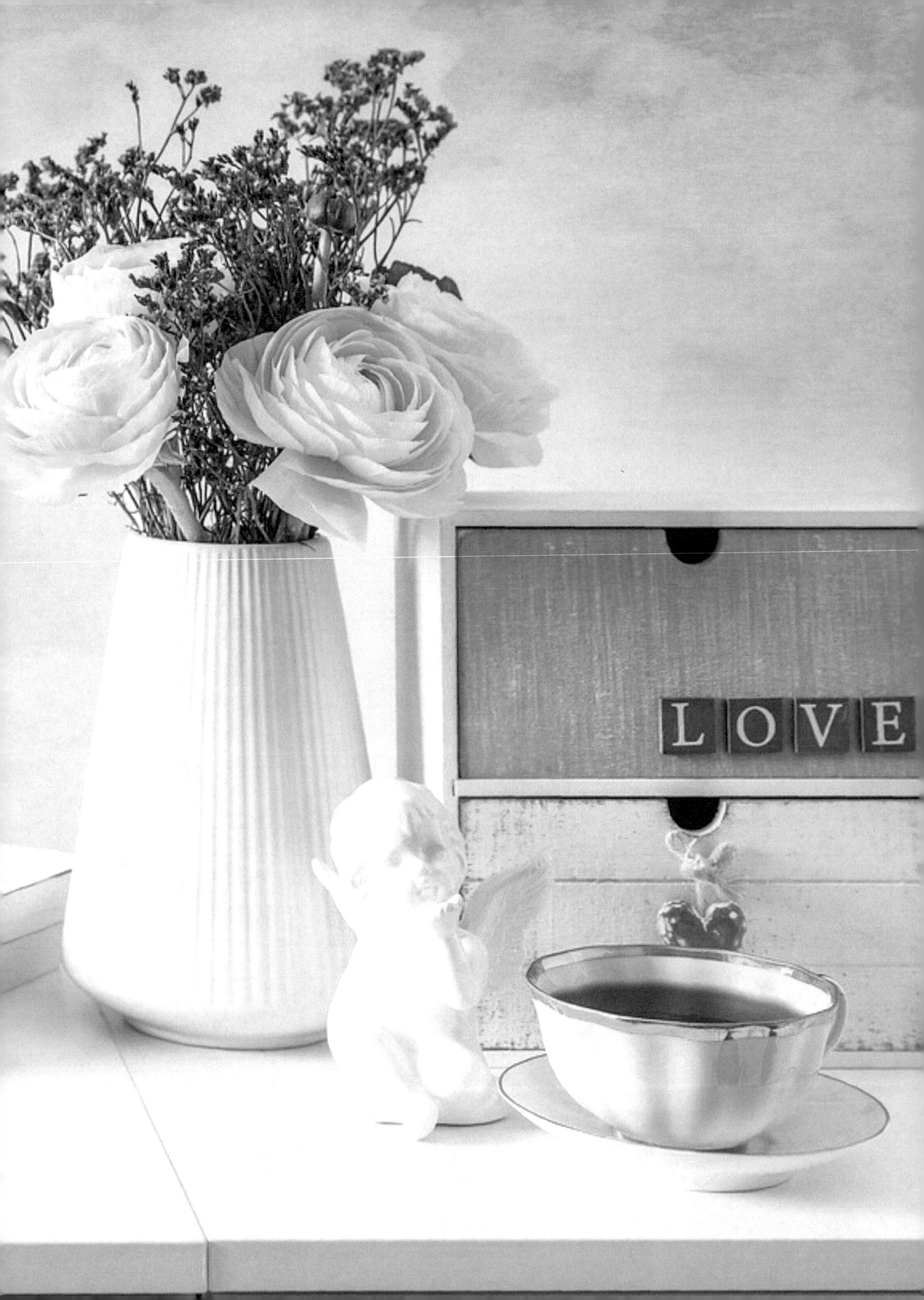
LOVE

I love MY FAMILY!

Family is where Life begins

Thank You

HAPPY

MOTHER

DAY

PRODUCTION

SCENE   TAKE

DIRECTOR

CAMERA

DATE

Made in United States
Troutdale, OR
12/30/2024

27432346R00097